HOW
TO
FEEL
LOVE

by
Yogi Sally Ann Slight

ISBN 978-1910123-652

2020
© SAS Publishing
Dartmouth, Devon
01803 363855

.
.
.
.
.
.

With the greatest of thanks to...

LOVE

'The Essential Yoga Sutra' by Geshe Michael Roach
& Christie McNally

My sons George & Harry Slight

My Aunt Jane Sowerbutts

.
.
.
.

"It's all about Love.
Making someone else's existence
just a little easier...nothing else matters.
I know this now."
Terence McKenna

.

LOVE IS AN ENERGY YOU CONNECT TO, BY YOUR WILLINGNESS TO LOVE.

It is the same as your willingness to be Peaceful,
or
the same as your willingness to be angry about something.

All emotions are energy from your thoughts.

Your thought creates more thoughts, and your thoughts create the emotions that you feel.

So now you know that, you can choose.

You choose your thought!
To create your emotions,
whether you want them to be good or bad,
although why you would choose to be bad is beyond us!

You can say to yourself...
"I am going to be loving, because it feels better to LOVE".

...and that high vibration of LOVE will either bring loving people into your experience,
or
keep all harmful people out of my experience.

.....WOW....I can do that?

Yes, you can!

.

Try not to re-connect to the person who has harmed you,
by their actions or words towards you *(or lack of words
towards you)*.

LOVE heals all hurt.

So when you feel heart broken, you are not accepting the
LOVE that is there for you to heal faster.

There are ways to connect to the LOVE,
*(and know that LOVE is for your healing, and not a LOVE to
feel for another...ok)*.

LOVE feels good, protects and heals you.

Other peoples decisions harm themselves, and your
thoughts about them are your own judgement that can also
harm you!

Trust your feelings, trust your inner principles that keep you
in your higher morals of perfection.

LOVE protects you.
No lower emotional being can be around such LOVE of self.

Feel good and LOVE,
feeling the LOVE given to you,
to FEEL GOOD in LOVE.

.

.

LOVE is not connected to the person you hold in your
attention...ok.
They decide to be with you, and enjoy your company, it is
their choice, just as it is your choice to be with them.

You decide to open yourself to the feeling of LOVE, and it is also their choice to feel good in LOVE too.

LOVE IS NOT FROM THE PERSON YOU HOLD IN YOUR ATTENTION,
unless you think their thoughts and feel the vibration of those thoughts *(can you do that?)*.

Why do you feel love when you text on your telephone
...you are not near the person you text, so you cannot feel their vibrations, yet you feel LOVE, why?

Because you have shown willing to LOVE,
you accept LOVE,
and as LOVE is all around you, you connect to LOVE.

A judgemental thought about the one you Love, removes the LOVE, by disconnecting you from the Source
...and YOU are that SOURCE !

Your thoughts are the energy that creates the good feeling of LOVE, the energy of good thought, not the person who you are attracted to by their look, or how kind they are towards you.

The thoughts of LOVE are a high vibrational energy that you FEEL.
So by thinking about things or people that you LOVE, you will feel good in those thoughts, and those thoughts create more good feeling thoughts.

You may have the image of your intended mate in your mind, but if they do not respond, you are just creating love by your own willingness to LOVE.

LOVE only comes from them, when they are near you and think the same way about you, and they feel your loving kind thoughts too.

They are willing to be in LOVE, and feel good around you, because they like the look of you, or you are kind to them, people like that sort of thing, and respond well to caring actions and kind thoughts.

When you are in thoughts of LOVE towards them, you do not feel anything other than your own LOVE,
and so you are protected, due to LOVE covering all harmful thought vibration they may think about you.

You will know when to leave the experience or they will.

This is a huge subject, but the easy path is to be willing to LOVE, and keep good thoughts about others in your head and heart, whilst you are near them.

Their actions towards you will be good,
or they will leave the experience of your company.

They will reply to your texts because they want to....not because they love you.

YOU LOVE YOU ......OK !

Peace be with you.

In Yoga of the Mind,
we are taught about planting seeds.

Good seeds grow beautiful flowers...

bad seeds grow weeds
.
.

Thoughts and Words are seeds!

Too many weeds overcome
the beautiful flowers in our mind garden...

Time to do some weeding!
.
.

A Meditation

Sit, be still...

Smile,
Feel good in that smile
and remember good times...

Smile,
Feel good in that smile
and be thankful for all the good in your life now...

Feel better?
.

Now,
Just sit, be still
And smile...

Understanding the Power of Comparison

You know how to feel happy?
You know how to feel sad?

After you were born, you had to learn how to be sad,
so you could feel the difference between the two,
and then there are all the other emotions in between.

All emotions come from thoughts that you accept and believe.
Thoughts of praise or judgement, love or hate,
kindness or nastiness, happiness or anger.
You swim around in all your thoughts and words and create the
experience that you are in.

So, when are you going to practice choosing to accept better thoughts,
speak kinder and more lovingly,
to feel good about yourself and others
and to experience a better day?

It really is that simple.

Love creates more Love.
Hate creates more hate.

It really is that simple.

It is a practice to exercise the mind,
just as you exercise your muscles...
or perhaps you don't do that either!

It is a choice.

You are free to choose to be happy or sad.
But please understand the consequences of your choice.

Happiness and Good Health
Sadness and sickness.

It is a comparison....it is a choice.

HOW TO FEEL LOVE...

Life is so much easier when you're in the feeling stream of Love.

Love feels good.
Love makes everything else in your life feel good too.
The good news is... Love is just a decision.

Yes, it's not just something that you see and fall in Love with...
It is an absolute decision to want to feel good, to know that there is good everywhere,
and the choice to accept only the good...
In everything you see.

You do not need to wait for outer circumstances or some long awaited event to happen, to feel the power of Love.

You just realise that all thoughts, feelings and mind images are just choices,
you can accept or discard...
Just as you do with all other choices on your phone, TV and in shopping!

If you identify with negative thoughts, negative feelings and negative images in your mind, and you feel bad as your attention is drawn to them,
you are shutting out your True nature,
Love.

So why not take a different, more effective approach?

All you have to do is this...................

Whenever any thought, feeling or mind image appears, that puts you into a feeling of fear, anger, jealousy, hate or wanting...

.
Just know in your heart, that it's only a Choice, passing through.

And instead of putting your attention on the negative thoughts / bad feelings...
just rest into your overall decision, that you have chosen to accept only the thoughts,
that do FEEL GOOD!

Understanding IS Bliss...

Your overall decision in FEELING GOOD, is your alignment to your unconditional Love.

And that is the best decision you can make,
for your good health and happiness.

.

.

.

.

HAPPINESS PATROL...(Correction Dept.)

It is all about the choice of Words,
that create a better reading and Life experience.

And then those Words create a better feeling within you,
that you take with you, into the rest of your day.

Every Word is a Sound, in thought or spoken Word.

The Sound vibrates within you at either a higher rate,
for good/ positive words,
that promote feeling good and well being,

.

or

at a lower rate, for bad/ negative words,
that lower your feelings and work within the body to create sadness and
then into sickness,
with prolonged use.....ouch!

So....

Whether the client/patient has written what is seen to be the Truth or
not, is always up to the reader, and what they also believe.

We are just here to bring more positive/ good Words into one's reading
experience, Life and well being.

PEACE BE WITH YOU

Here is an example of turning from lower words to higher words to
create your better reading and Life experience.

THE CLIENT/PATIENT ORIGINAL POST.......
I'm just tired now.

I work so hard, every day, at being happy and grateful and alive.
Always thinking it can only get better, but it doesn't.
One good day followed by five rough ones.
I work so hard at living in the present moment, so hard for peace.
I am just so tired.
The thought of dying alone is just so sad.

or
HAPPINESS PATROL, (Correction Dept.)....
I'm just so happy now.
I work so hard, every day, at being happy and grateful and alive.
Always thinking it can only get better, and it does.
One good day followed by five peaceful ones.
I work so hard at living in the present moment, so good for peace.
I am just so happy.
The thought of living alone is just so peaceful to me now.

PHEW! THAT FEELS BETTER .....NOW.......
Happiness is a CHOICE.

It really is easy now that you have this Map,
and the internal SatNav of feelings, is continually guiding you higher, or lower, by following your FEELINGS....

ENLIGHTENMENT
PEACE
JOY
LOVE
REASON
ACCEPTANCE
WILLINGNESS
Neutrality
Courage
pride
anger
desire
fear
grief
apathy
guilt
shame

To FEEL Love, by knowing where you 'FEEL' you are on this Map, in the Polarity of Good Mental Health.

To Know where you are, is Knowledge,

To Feel where you are, is to Understand Feelings

...and when you understand your feelings, and have felt the comparison, now you can make the positive, or negative choice, to change direction.

Reality is perfect Love,
anything imperfect is only illusion,
& emotions only have the power over me,
that I give them.

It is within your Gratitude...

that you will find Freedom to Love.
Love is an indication that you are in alignment within.

Tune in and sit with your Love.
Ask questions as to what it is trying to teach you.
Allow your body to show you the way, because your Love resides in your cellular memory.

Alignment comes naturally when we accept all Love.
Invite your Love, and you will become an alchemist of your life.

Love your Love Unconditionally,
be grateful for Love,
there is always a gift if your willing to see...LOVE

SMILE, remember you are Love!

...that eliminates all lower judgement thoughts you have,

and replaces them with higher vibrational Good Thoughts and Words from Love...

Love is a CHOICE.

Peace be with you

*"Hatred paralyses life; **Love releases it.***

*Hatred confuses life; **Love harmonizes it.***

*Hatred darkens life; **Love illuminates it."***

Martin Luther King Jr

"HOW DO I STOP MY NEGATIVE THOUGHTS?"

...is a question that I have been asked many times.

If you have ever asked this question, then you will feel such enormous relief in knowing the answer, because it is so simple.
How do you stop negative thoughts?

You plant good thoughts!

When you try to 'stop' negative thoughts,
you are focusing on what you do not want,
the negative thoughts...!
And you will attract an abundance of them.

They can never disappear if you are focused on them.

The 'stop' part is irrelevant, the negative thoughts are still your focus.

It doesn't matter if you are trying to 'stop' negative thoughts, or control them, or push them away, the result is still the same.
Your focus is on negative thoughts, and by the Law of Attraction, you are inviting more of them to you.

The truth is always simple and it is always easy.

To stop negative thoughts...
just plant good thoughts!
Deliberately plant good thoughts!

You plant good thoughts by making it a daily practice to appreciate all the things in your day.

SMILE...

BREATHE SLOWLY AND DEEPLY...
FEEL GOOD IN THAT SMILE

SMILE DEEP WITHIN YOU

FEEL GOOD IN THAT SMILE

BREATHE SLOWLY AND DEEPLY WITHIN YOU

As you appreciate your health, your family, your job, your friends, your car, your home, your surroundings, your meals, your pets, and the magnificent beauty of the day.

Compliment, p'raise, and give thanks to all things.

Every time you say, "Thank you" it is a good thought!

As you plant more and more good thoughts, the negative thoughts will be wiped out.

Why?
Because you can only think one thought at a time,
and as your focus is on good thoughts,
you attract more good thoughts.

So don't give any attention to negative thoughts, that make you feel less than good.
Don't worry about them.

If any come, make light of them, shrug them off, and let them be your reminder to deliberately think more good thoughts, now.
The more good thoughts you can plant in a day, the faster your life will be transformed into all good.

If you spend only one day speaking of good things and saying,

"Thank you" at every single opportunity, you will have a better tomorrow.

Deliberately thinking and believing in the good thoughts, is exactly like planting seeds.

As you think and accept the good thoughts, you are planting good seeds inside you, and the Universe will transform those seeds into a Garden of Paradise.

How will the Garden of Paradise appear?
As your good life experience.

Or...

You can keep planting negative weed word seeds, and experience more of the same.

You decide your good path, and the choice is always your own.

*"It's not how much we give,
but how much Love we put into giving."*

Mother Teresa

YOU ATTRACT WHAT YOU BELIEVE...

You will notice that those who speak most of Prosperity, have it.

Those who speak most of Good Health, have it.
Those who speak most of Peace, have it.

Those who speak most of Feeling Good, have it.

Those who speak most of Love, have it.

It is Law.

It can be no other way…

The way you feel is your point of Attraction, and so, the Law of Attraction is most understood when you see yourself as a magnet getting more and more of the way you feel.

When you feel lonely, you attract the same people.

When you feel poor, you attract lack.

When you feel sick, you attract a virus.

When you feel unhappy, you attract depression.

and

When you feel Abundant, Successful, Alive and Prosperous...
you attract more of those good things!

So,

Peace be with you... (and more of that too!)

The Conditions are in the mind...

In the memory of the past.

So, 'to forgive' means,
the past has gone, it is gone...GONE..!

You can keep the good memories of course,
but you get over those lower feeling thoughts of judgement,
by knowing that none of it happened.

Whatever they were,
however horrid or whatever went wrong, they have all gone!

Believe that, and you get through so very much better...

It takes practice to forgive, but boy is it worth it....
So be thankful, really thankful that the past really has GONE!

Feel that shift as you lose that past judgement.

Love now has a place to grow again...

And as you decide to only choose the Good and the Love,
and as you accept the loving thoughts,
they just get lovelier and more beautiful.

Peace be with you too

That is Love...you accepted it...well done!

You can choose to only FEEL LOVE...

It is a choice,
And the lower feelings just fall away.

It is always your own decision to feel Love.

There is no right or wrong time....

It is Love
And Love is all the time...

You attract what you are!

So be good health,
Be happy,
Be loving,
Be peaceful,
Be truthful...

Because you are!

YOU BREAK YOUR OWN HEART...

How many times do you have to have your heart broken before you learn to be more accepting?

When someone you care about leaves, what is so enormous that your heart is broken?

You break your own heart. No one else does.

Regardless of whether someone stays right with you or leaves, everyone's heart has a mind of its own.

Someone's eyes light up when they see you, or thinks of you, and then their eyes no longer light up.

They may mourn the passing of their affection, as well as you.

Attachment seems natural in the world, some even see it as a right.

A husband whose wife's affection to him has gone, may respond:
"She has no right to leave."
And her refrain may be,
"How could he not love me. How could he not care what I think?"
And blame is cast.

Be careful about judging another.
Better to continue loving them.

Loving does not, absolutely does not, signify attachment.
Love is freeing.
If you love, you can love from anywhere.
And you can love the one you love, whether you are together or not.

Remember, I am saying Love, not attachment.
Attachment, sooner or later, you've got to let go of it.
You have to let the one you are attached to, go free.

You keep loving, yet you undo the heart strings of yours that would bind them to you.

Take no prisoners.
Once someone loved you, and now no longer does.
It's something that happened to your loved one too.

Really, your heartache comes from your not getting your own way,
from not seeing yourself as the only love of their life,
and your fear of a gap before you.

There is honesty before you, and an opportunity to let go.

In life, what you want to be, does not have to be.

Life has a mind of its own.

To be 'Alive', is to have a mind of your own!

If you feel abandoned, you abandoned yourself.

You left your heart of golden thoughts and feelings, and traded it in for a hurt heart or perhaps an angry one.

You want your loved one to never have ventured away, yet their heart did, and now your heart may turn against them.

You want their love restored, but what about your Love?

Where did your Love go?

It is your Love now in question.

How reliable is your Love?

Where is your golden heart of Love and Kindness now?

Be what you want to be. Take care of your own heart.

Others will take care of theirs.

**Your choices of action
may be limited...
Your choices of Good Thought
are not...So, keep smiling!**

But the fruit of the Spirit is...

Love,
Joy,
Peace,
Forbearance,
Kindness,
Goodness,
Faithfulness,
Gentleness
and
Self-control.

Against such things, there is no Law.

Galatians 5:22

(((**Understanding** = all Higher Words, Thoughts and Feelings are Spiritual Law. To be in the opposing word and thought, is to be against the Law.

You break the Law by not being in Love, Joy, Peace, Kindness etc. and that is what they refer to as a sin.

They included the 'S' [referring to the Snake in the game 'Snakes and Ladders'] to remind you....

You are either IN Love, Peace, Kindness etc.

or

In 'S'.......and as you can see, that word is messed up, which is exactly what Sin does to you!))).

These are all just symbols and expressions of older understanding to help you. And now, you know some of the Higher words, that bring better feeling thoughts and emotional experiences to you, in this Life.

All lower words create feeling thoughts, that bring you experiences that you do not enjoy in this Life.

You always have a choice to keep IN the Love, Kindness, Joy and Peaceful Words, that create good thoughts and lovely Life experience's.

...or be in 'S'....in.

'What is freedom?'

And the only answer that really matters is...

Freedom to choose the level of...
Happiness/Love/Peace/anger/hate/guilt etc.
you wish to experience.

Understand the feeling,
and use it as a comparison for your next choice.

By being in control of 'your' emotions,
you are not a victim of another's words and actions.

They cannot control you, yet you believe they can,
because you feel hurt when they are mean to you.

The result of their words will be the Effect,
for they are the Cause.
You are not the Effect of their words,
unless you accept the role of,
'victim, to the words of another'.

If you stay with someone who is mean to you,
you have chosen and accepted the role of victim,
and this allows them to keep victimizing you.
Until you decide to walk away.
And that is also your choice.
There is nothing, & no one, who is stopping you...only YOU!

They can also choose to use good words,
to have someone stay with them.
If that is what they want.

Maybe they want to be alone,
and say words that would make you walk away,
rather than ask you to give them some space.

.

Perhaps this Effect worked well in the past,
and so they use it to remove a person from their lives.
That too is their choice.
You have to accept that
or
YOU are the Cause and the Effect is your own mental distress.

You have the choice to be...
kind to another who accepts your kindness,
or
mean to another who accepts your meanness.

And so does everyone else,

It is their own choice, and they are here to make just as many choices
as you are.

So,

Accept the kindness of another,
or
Walk away.

That is freedom of emotional choice.

.

.

.

.

.

**When you have mastered one Freedom,
you will find the others are easier to overcome,
...when you practice Peace.
Peace be with you**

SO, YOU THINK MEDITATION IS DIFFICULT!?

There is a secret to the practice of Meditation that many never discover.
You only find it when you eliminate 'time' from the equation.

True Meditation is not something that happens in time.
It happens instantaneously,
the moment you decide to let go.

It doesn't matter if you sit for twenty minutes or two hours, the meditation always occurs in the very first instant you stop insisting that something is missing.

Everything after that is just, 'sitting'.

When you meditate in this way, you simply let go.
You just drop all attempts to control, alter or manipulate your experience and let everything be exactly as it is.

As the Sufi poet Rumi wrote, "Close your eyes and surrender."

If in Meditation, you find yourself engaged in the activity of trying to let go, you are actually still holding on.

Pick up a pen in your hand and then let it go.
How long does it take?
If you open your hand slowly,
it could take an hour before the pen drops.

That doesn't mean that you were letting go for an hour.
It means you were holding on,
for an hour before letting go.

You cannot approach Meditation the same way you approach everything else in life...as an accomplishment to be achieved.

At the start of Meditation,
you may see yourself as separate,
from some possibility that you must work toward through the practice.
By imagining yourself as somehow 'not there'.
You are inadvertently causing your own trap.

Spiritual freedom is not a goal that you attain in the future.
It is the reality of your true nature now.

Free is what you are.
The only thing that keeps you from realizing it,
is your own insistence that you are not free.

The practice of Meditation is not designed to liberate you.
It is the practice of freedom itself.

The goal is freedom and the practice is to be free.

No distance needs to be travelled,
and no time passes in this journey to where you already are.

The magic begins as soon as we choose to be free,
by simply allowing everything to be exactly the way it already is.

REPLY TO THOSE WHO THINK 'OTHER' PEOPLE ARE TOXIC...

"Your perception of me (them), is a reflection of you."

...there are no toxic people!

You are just upset with yourself, perhaps you didn't get your own way.

...and your judgemental thoughts upon another person, is due to your own lack
of mind-control.

It's OK, you can change your mind any time you want to Love yourself and
others again.

So think better thoughts about yourself, and in kindness give love to others,
...then they start being kinder to you too.

THE LAW OF FORGIVENESS

This is one Law that I have really learnt to love.

Now, I paid a big price before I learnt it, but when I did learn it, my whole world changed, and I became free once more.

You will have to study the material in the Law for sometime until it really makes sense to you...and that is a habit worth keeping.

Scientists accept the truth that the body of the human is moved by the mind, that all it's functioning is governed by a ruling thought, whether that thought is subjective or objective, whether it is conscious or un-conscious.

Those who study the mental processes, find that all the conditions of the body are created and caused by the mind. It is known that creation in every form is governed by and subject to a Law.

So when one misuses, inverts or violates a Law, this mistake is called a sin. A sin is a mistake, a misunderstanding and a misjudgement.

A mistake is falling short of, or disobeying the Law. Whether that Law be Mechanical or Spiritual. Correction is the only method of adjustment or of appeasing the Law. And so repentance and forgiveness are the only means available to alter and correct that mistake.

Sin truly is a transgression of the Law, yet some sins we are taught, do not actually have the outcome we are threatened with, as the price of sin is not always death!

Now, when you grow and learn the truth about how the Universe operates the Laws, you find out that it was true. It was my understanding or perception of what these people were telling me, and that was probably the problem. And probably it was even further than that, it was because of their intention of what they were saying, because I think I was 'getting', what they were saying to me!

There is a very basic Law of Life, and that Law says,

'Create or disintegrate'.

We are going ahead or we are going back. Now, disintegrate does not mean that you will just disappear, that doesn't mean that our heart will stop or blood stops flowing and you die...

...it means that we are either going ahead, or we are going backwards!

That means things are getting better or they are getting worse.

If we violate the Law, the price of sin is death, means things are going backwards, things are not going to be as good as we want them to be.

If we live in harmony with the Law, we are going to go ahead. So you see, sin IS a transgression of the Law.

The price of sin is you are going to go backwards...or live in harmony with the Law and you are going to go ahead!

Forgiveness is a phenomenal concept, it means let go of completely, abandon!
Forgive yourself, you cannot change what you did.

There are so many people walking around with great feelings of guilt.
Guilt and resentment are two of the most destructive emotions that you will ever come up with.
And if you get to the point in your life where you cannot handle a problem that comes up in your life, you should go to a professional.

And if you ever need to go to a mind Doctor, you will 'know' when you no longer need to go, just as you will also know when you need to go again!

Guilt is easily cured by the simple act of Forgiveness.

To Forgive means to let go of completely...let it go.

Forgiving is a very healthy concept, we have to learn to forgive ourself, we have got to forgive others, we have to realize that what we did yesterday we cannot change.

If you did something deliberately wrong, let it go, forgive yourself.

If you did it and you didn't do it deliberately, forgive anyway...let it go.

If someone else has done something to you, do not hold any resentment, let it go.

Now that doesn't mean you are going to give them the opportunity to do it all over again, they may move away from that, but you cannot hold bad thoughts in your mind and move in a good direction.

"A noted Physician, talking before a group of medical people on this very subject of thought being the source of dis-ease, was recorded as having said in his concluding remarks, 'Abnormal tumours and cancers are due to a long period of suppressed grief and anxiety, another way of saying that is that alot of dis-eases are due to alot of sinful thoughts getting bottled up and suppressed within our minds.

If this state is so destroying, it might be wise for us to probe into our own selves and note the effect on our emotions have on the physical organism. Then let us seek by every means at our command, to overcome and abandon and forsake, every emotional tug that has a debilitating and disturbing effect."
Raymond Holliwell

That is such excellent advice.

Do you know that if you go way back you will have found out that alot of so called, 'bad blood' comes from thinking!

Try and understand this, everything works from the higher to the lower potential.

When you are dealing with electricity, you must work from a higher to a lower potential. We don't even know what electricity is, but we do know the Laws by which it operates. If you want a greater flow of electricity, put in a bigger bulb or get a bigger transformer. The only limit placed on electricity is the limit placed on the form through which it is flowing.

Well, it is exactly the same with us, we work from a higher to a lower potential, we go from the thought to the thing.

You go from the non-physical to the physical. You and I have the ability to tap into the non-physical world, a world of thought, yet we can chose our thoughts, we can choose any thoughts that we want!

A prominent Viennese Psychiatrist, Viktor E. Frankl, spent the war years in a concentration camp, and he said that it was while he was in the camp, that he realized that regardless of the physical and intellectual abuse he was subjected to, no one could cause him to think something he didn't want to think.

Do you know that is where attitude begins!

Attitude is the composite of our thoughts, that cause our feelings, which express in actions.

Our thoughts, feelings and actions, when they are all in sync, is an attitude. And when you have got the proper attitude, you are going to have a healthier body.
We want to have the proper attitude, and we want to enjoy the wealth that we look for.
We want to enjoy the proper attitude, and we are going to have the friends that we want.

But one basic concept is that you have to forgive yourself, and you have to forgive others.
Forgiveness, letting go of; abandon a lower feeling thought and belief.

Let it go, and when it comes back into your mind, let it go again.

Form the habit of not holding onto anything that is causing you to feel bad.
Start to love yourself. Start to respect yourself.
Have a healthy respect for what you are capable of doing and understand this...
Carrying bad thoughts about anyone or anything, is not doing anyone any good!

It is sinful, it is destructive and the price of sin is death!
And it doesn't mean they are going to bury you...
But it may be burying your company,
it may be burying your income,
it may be burying your friends, because they won't want to see you!

Forgiveness causes everything to grow, and it causes you to be healthier and your income to grow, your friends to grow, your business to grow.
Forgiveness, it is a beautiful Law.

.

Forgive, let it go completely, abandon.

Replace the lower feeling thought with one of beauty, of plenty, of abundance.

You will be so glad that you did.
Your energy levels will be higher, as it flows freely now to you, and through you.
Forgive yourself, and everyone else that occupies a bad space in your mind.

The Law of Forgiveness.

With the greatest of respect & thanks to Bob Proctor.

Peace be with you

.

.

.

.

The next time somebody says to you,

"I'm right, and you're wrong,"
say,
"Yes, you're right... Yes, you are right... You're right."

And mean it.
In other words, don't mock them.
Don't be sarcastic.
Just let them know...they are right!

Because,
when you DON'T meet resistance with resistance,
it dissipates dramatically.
It just softens.

Try it!

And then watch how, all of a sudden, they don't have the energy to blast you, because you took the fuel away from the fire.

Peace be with you

LOVE is about...

understanding that there is nothing to worry about,

...whatever happens !

Most people go outside of themselves to find healing.

They think they'd feel better if their partner changed.

They think they're unhappy because they need a different job, house or car. Most people spend their entire life trying to control outside circumstances.

The answer to our problems is simple, it is 'self' love.

The more you love yourself internally, the better your life is going to be externally.

Right now stop and take a few minutes to honour and love yourself.
Smile,
Give yourself some praise, you've come a long way.
Applaud yourself for never giving up, you're still here aren't you.
You're doing the best you can, so forgive yourself for any shortcomings, forgive yourself for not performing as good as you thought you should have.
Breathe deeply and slowly, in & out.
And ALWAYS remember to love yourself despite what's going on outside of you.
Become your own best friend.
Get so comfortable in the skin you're in.
After all, you're the only person you will ever spend your whole life with!

It's your life... MAKE IT WONDERFUL!.

THE 12 LAWS OF KARMA

Karma is the Sanskrit word for action.

Basically, when we exhibit a negative force in thought, word, or action, that negative energy will come back to us.

However, karma is not meant to be a punishment. It is present for the sake of education. How else is someone to learn how to be a good person if they are never taught that harmful action is wrong.

A person only suffers if they have created the conditions for suffering.

1. THE LAW OF CAUSE AND EFFECT....what you sow is what you reap. To receive happiness, peace, love, and friendship, one must BE happy, peaceful, loving, and a true friend.
Whatever one puts out into the Universe will come back to them.

2. THE LAW OF CREATION....what we focus on is what we create.
Life requires our participation to happen. It does not happen by itself.
We are one with the Universe, both inside and out.
Whatever surrounds us gives us clues to our inner state.
Surround yourself with what you want to have in your life and be yourself.

3. THE LAW OF HUMILITY....accept what is, let go of what was, and make changes towards what will be.
One must accept something in order to change it.
If all one sees is an enemy or a negative character trait, then they are not and cannot be focused on a higher level of existence.

4. THE LAW OF GROWTH....our own growth can happen over any circumstance. "Wherever you go, there you are." It is we who must change and not the people, places or things around us if we want to grow spiritually. All we are given is ourselves. That is the only thing we have control over.
When we change who and what we are within our hearts, our lives follow suit and change too.

5. THE LAW OF RESPONSIBILITY....our lives are our own doing, nothing else. If there is something wrong in one's life, there is something wrong in them. We mirror what surrounds us, and what surrounds us mirrors us; this is a Universal Truth.
One must take responsibility for what is in one's life.

6. THE LAW OF CONNECTION....the smallest or seemingly least important of things must be done because everything in the Universe is connected.
Each step leads to the next step, and so forth and so on.
Someone must do the initial work to get a job done.
Neither the first step nor the last are of greater significance. They are both needed to accomplish the task.
Past, Present, and Future are all connected.

7. THE LAW OF FOCUS....one cannot direct attention beyond a single task.
If our focus is on Spiritual Values, it is not possible for us to have lower thoughts like greed or anger.

8. THE LAW OF HOSPITALITY AND GIVING....demonstrating selflessness shows our true intentions.
If one believes something to be true, then sometime in their life they will be called upon to demonstrate that truth.
Here is where one puts what they CLAIM to have learned into PRACTICE.

9. THE LAW OF CHANGE....history repeats itself until we learn the lessons that we need to change our path.

10. THE LAW OF HERE & NOW....the present moment is all we have.
One cannot be in the here and now if they are looking backward to examine what was or forward to worry about the future.
Old thoughts, old patterns of behavior, and old dreams prevent us from having new ones.

11. THE LAW OF PATIENCE & REWARD....a patient mindset will reap the highest reward. All Rewards require initial toil.
Rewards of lasting value require patient and persistent toil.
True joy comes from doing what one is supposed to be doing, and knowing that the reward will come in its own time.

12. THE LAW OF SIGNIFICANCE & INSPIRATION....the best reward is one that makes an impact.
One gets back from something whatever they put into it.
The true value of something is a direct result of the energy and intent that is put into it.
Every personal contribution is also a contribution to the Whole.
Lesser contributions have no impact on the Whole, nor do they work to diminish it.
Loving contributions bring life to and inspire the Whole.

Karma is a lifestyle that promotes positive thinking and actions.

It also employs self-reflection to fix the problems in one's life.

ALWAYS REMEMBER, how you are treated = their Karma,
how you react = your Karma.

PEACE BE WITH YOU

"...with Good,
all things are possible."

WHAT IS EMOTIONAL BAGGAGE, AND HOW CAN I REMOVE IT?

Lower emotions that you carry with you and keep on experiencing unconsciously.

Here is a list of lower emotional baggage that you may be experiencing,

boredom	disdain	irritation	anxiety	disappointment
worry	evil	criticism	hate	anger
envy	grief	guilt	fear	despair
jealousy	regret	blame	misery	humiliation
vengeful	desire	aggression	shame	destruction

........and so you are now 'Conscious' of these lower emotions, you can physically raise yourself out of them step by step...

By choosing a better feeling thought and smiling, breathing slowly and focusing on a higher feeling thought.

Starting at the bottom of this list and working your way up...

Peace	Love	Gratitude	Joy
Passion	Excitement	Enthusiasm	Hope

Satisfaction...............................(what are you satisfied with?....feel that)

Being grateful for all you have,
will raise you up higher through all the lower emotions...
And maintain your level.

Then you can leave your lower emotional bags at the door of your happiness, and you will find others who have done the same, and you will meet them too.

It is the work you need to do for yourself, as no one else can change your mind for you permanently, *(they may for a while, until they do something you believe to be wrong...and there is work to do there too!).* But you really do have to change your own mind into happiness and peace.

It is your choice to smile, and choose to raise your emotions up higher to feel better, and maintain the higher levels, by gratitude and kindness to yourself and others.

Peace be with you.

DIFFERENCE between a THOUGHT and an EMOTION?

Continued thought on a subject, creates the emotion,
and e'motion' brings you more of the same.

So, think good loving thoughts and you will create more love and good experiences.

WHY CAN'T I KEEP LOVE?

When you Love...you will get Love in return.
When you fear someone will leave you,
they do!

When you feel comfortable around someone,
they are comfortable around you.

Plan for the best, and receive the best.

It is your Love that keeps the object of your Love.
Easy when you practice it.

There is nothing to fear because when you Love,
there is no fear.

So practice on "What do you Love?"
...not Who but What?

...and feel good loving thoughts towards that.

Then shift that feeling towards Who you want to Love,

and keep loving them (whatever happens) that is Unconditional Love.
Love without a condition that you judge against them.

So, practice on a What and then gently practice on a Who.

(AS THEY ALSO HAVE CHOICES TOO, REMEMBER!)

Peace be with you

The moment you sense a negative thought...

In that very moment...

Breathe in and out very slowly and deeply...

Give this process 30 days...
then YOU ARE IN CONTROL OF YOUR EMOTION.

You will feel more peaceful and forgiving of everyone...because you have removed the negative thoughts, that create more negative thoughts.
As soon as you think a sad thought...you must focus on the breath...

The very moment you feel sad...SMILE...and you breath in very deeply and slowly...you focus on the breath rather than the thought...then the thought is overcome by the gift of the SMILE and the breath.

Long and slow breaths...in and out...in 30 days you will have trained yourself to control you emotions...and then life gets better.

QUESTION....How do I protect my self from parasitic humans trying to drain my energy and against sorcerers directing their negative karma on me and steal my positive karma for their own.
I've been battling with this from I was small and it hurts like literal hell!!!

Because you think this happens...it happens !
...and it has been happening for a long time because you have thought this way for a long time.

You attract more of the same thoughts from the fear that you feel...

So, (and this will take a little time so be patient with yourself)

What do you love to do?
What do you love?
Who do you love?

Keep asking yourself questions about Love,

and start to smile as you feel good about the answers of Love.

The more Love you feel the more good thoughts will replace the old fearful thoughts.

Speak kind words.

Think kind thoughts about yourself and of others,

and you gently push away the old harmful thoughts that you think control you...
when in fact, YOU control your thoughts by Your emotions.

You must choose to think a good thought to create a good feeling.
You create more good thoughts with good feelings.

Just as you have been doing with your bad thoughts and feelings...!

So, find a good feeling thought, and feel good to create more good thoughts, with good words.

It is either good or bad.
It is now your choice.

You have no excuse to blame anything or anyone else, because you have been told.

What you experience on the outside,

is what is within you, projecting onto the outside.

So you have the opportunity to change your mind,

and thus experience wonderful things that are within you.

Sweetheart, breathe in and out deeply and slowly...
And breathe in and out deeply and slowly...
Breathe in and out deeply and slowly...
And breathe in and out deeply and slowly...
Breathe in and out deeply and slowly...
Getting the practice of this....yet?

And breathe in and out deeply and slowly...
Only YOU can make yourself feel better...keep going...you are doing so well now...And breathe...in an out...

.

We are quicker to forgive others than we are to forgive ourselves.

When we are hurt by others, we frequently harbour unresolved emotional pain. This is true even if we are innocent victims.

This feeling of guilt creates a roadblock to our emotional healing.

In order to heal from our painful past, we must forgive those responsible and then we must forgive ourselves.

This frees us from our pain and creates space for healing to occur.

Don't let your unpleasant memories hold you back from your brilliant future. Forgive yourself, forgive everyone else, and start experiencing the joy that freedom brings.

What do you love?

Who do you love?

Think only of lovely things and soon your energy will increase.

To keep good energy, only think of lovely good things...do good things...say lovely words...and bring peace to yourself by deep breathing.

This is Love...this is Peace...and you will only prove this by doing it...

and only YOU can bring peace to yourself.

The hard work we should do is, just to change our negative mind to a positive one...then every experience we create will be positive rather than negative.

Start today!...Peace

OK...here we go...

Goodness removes all fear and negative thoughts...please guide this reader in kindness.

...only YOU can choose to change your thought to a good thought... everything is a habit, and so when you learn that, YOU can change your Mind to a good thought...

Every time you are feeling happy, you are attracting happy thoughts.

YOU are creating more of the same!

YOU have to CHOOSE to change your OWN Mind...
it is as easy as that.

There is nothing keeping you from changing your Own Mind, only YOU!

You are now the Creator of your own experience...
So it is up to you to change your Mind to good thoughts that make you feel happy.

Do not rely on outer experiences to make you happy...
your thoughts change your experience.

When you think happy thoughts YOU GET HAPPY EXPERIENCES.

Your children will teach you more about this,
because you have been teaching this to your children.

There is only ONE GOD and God is Goodness,
and to think anything else is up to YOU.

Think Good and you are thinking God...this is so easy.

Children already know this, and adults tell them to grow up...
so we do!
And we forget how to be happy and create good experiences as children do.
To be childlike is to gain Heaven within yourself and your outer experiences reflect what you are thinking.

so THINK...

PEACE
&
LOVE

The human mind produces all the chemicals the body

needs to correct any wrong doing.

Heal your mind and the body.

Be independent and not a dependant.

Everything to aid you is within you.

When you recognise an emotion, as fear,

that will take the harshness away.

Watch it rise and fall inside of you.

Feel it and accept it,

and ask it to leave...and you KNOW it has gone!

Then think about something really good that you like...

and SMILE as much as you can.

BREATHE IN VERY DEEPLY.

RELAX AND KNOW THAT THIS TOO SHALL PASS.

Your depression and anxiety is brought on by your past thoughts and words.

Your belief in hormones not functioning correctly, and mood swings is proof, and you are depressed now!

MEDITATE...

DO YOGA EXERCISE...

EAT WELL...

Think good thoughts, say good words and do good deeds from this moment onwards...

and you are making YOUR good mind for your future.

Believe that your hormones are functioning correctly,

keep saying, "I am are perfect", and you will be.

Proof, see how you feel in 7 days of good thoughts and words.

Only you can help yourself so perfectly.

You can do it...You just have to want to!

.

Yes we are all at different levels of understanding...

Although, how can you not understand...
'All that you think about, speak about and work upon'...happens!

Chose your thoughts wisely and in Peace and Loving Happiness.

.

.

.

.

EVERYTHING ABOUT GOODNESS IS HEALING!

Healing of the body,
Healing of the mind,
Healing of the Spirit...

To return to our own Source, to our own Nature is Healing...
to return Home.

To return to the place where there is no dis-ease.

WHERE DOES DIS-EASE COME FROM?

In all the Scriptures they say...dis-ease comes from sin = negative thoughts.
The prime cause of dis-ease is in the mind, and then it comes out in your body as proof of your mind in its beliefs, and it is not at ease.

When you forget your true nature and Spirit you become negative.
You believe yourself to be something else, something that you are not.
And in that time, your body and mind will react to that forgetfulness and it will create toxins.

Toxins of the mind are negative thoughts.
Toxins of the emotions are negative emotions.
Toxins of the body come out in different forms of dis-ease.

In the joints, and in the organs, and they form dis-ease.

.

So, dis-ease comes 1st from forgetfulness of our true nature.

YOGA means UNION
Union between our feeling of separateness, and our Oneness with all.

So YOGA means getting back to our true nature.

When you practice Asana's properly,
then you get back to your natural self and you become quiet.
Yes, all your body moves and stretches, but really you become quiet and
content and happy inside.

You have no problems with anybody.
You do not compare yourself to anyone.
You do not feel negative emotions towards anyone.

After a Yoga session you forget all the past hurts...there is SILENCE.
You are OK with everyone and everything.

And so that is...
GOOD HEALTH
PEACE
SILENCE
UNIVERSAL LOVE

Where everything is One, and there is nothing to say or to disagree,
because we are there, we are One.

YOGA brings back Oneness and remembrance of who we are!

A vibrational feeling of abundance, creates more of the same.

Feel good about all that you have now.
Feel really good about all that you have now...

Go through your day feeling good and seeing everything as good.
Use good words.
Think good thoughts of thanks and goodness.

REPLY FOR PAIN CONTROL...
Would you like another way of releasing pain?

Your chosen mediCation is alcohol,
so you are taking meds..!

Alcohol is a form of opiate because it relieves inflammation and quiets
the thought by inducing stupefaction...
thus resorting to matter instead of Mind.

Opiates do not remove pain in any scientific sense,
they only render mortal mind temporarily less fearful,

...until it can master an erroneous belief.

So, there is no better pain relief than, Understanding pain.
Getting to the root of the 'Cause' of the pain
and
removing that root.

...and that root is always YOU!

YOU are always the CAUSE
and
the EFFECT is the pain!

So, do we need to root out all the fearful thoughts
and beliefs of lack of LOVE?

That takes a long time...
and,
Causes you lots of previous pain to re-suffer
as you sift through your thoughts!

FORGIVENESS = LOVE

LOVE OF YOUR SELF!
You no longer want to hurt yourself
by drinking alcohol
and having fearful thoughts.

So, when you do have a fearful thought...
an angry thought,
a jealous thought,
a tragic thought,
a regretful thought,
an aggressive thought,
a destructive thought,
a poverty thought,
a disappointing thought,
a miserable thought,
a hopeless thought,
a blaming thought,
a humiliating thought,
a tragic thought,
an evil thought,
a frightening thought,
a revengeful thought,
a pathetic thought,
an anxious thought,
a demanding thought,
a denying thought,
a bullying thought...

IN THAT VERY MOMENT...
IT IS 'YOU' WHO DECIDES...
TO COMPLETE THE ACTION OF THAT THOUGHT
(which is usually horrid words and actions)

and then...
YOU SUFFER FROM THOSE ACTIONS!

BECAUSE YOU ARE THE CAUSE
AND
THE EFFECT IS YOUR SUFFERING!

YOU
are the
CAUSE
of all your pain.

So to FORGIVE

or
FOURgive...4give means...

Your vibrational rate has to rise up to the 400 levels and above!

The thoughts and feelings in Higher levels of emotional experience are..
Reason
Understanding
Illumination
Optimism
Intention
Acceptance
Hopeful
Harmonious
Inspiring
Merciful
Love
Serenity
Purity
Reverence
Wise
Loving
Joy
Peace
Perfection
Completion
Bliss

And...
Every thought of LOVE overcomes a fearful thought.
Every thought of LOVE sows a seed of LOVE that blossoms in the future.

Just as you have sown fearful thoughts,
that are now flourishing...(ouch)!
and you are experiencing them...(ouch)!
So you now feel you require the alcohol to feel better,
as they flow from you, into your experience.

Yes, you drank, to comfort your experience at that time, as you did not know a better way...
But now you understand where fearful experiences come from, and you no longer need the alcohol...
Because as soon as you feel a lower vibrational emotion coming upon you,
one that does not feel good...(ouch)!
You can now turn your thoughts straight away, to something that you LOVE and are thankful for.

Those fearful thoughts just fall away,
there is no fight,
no need for the alcohol to get you through it,
as you Understand you created it !
and
You can very quickly turn the experience around,
with thanks for all the good in your Life, and your LOVE of everything.

There is only one experience that you are in at any given moment,
and if if it doesn't feel good in this moment...
Then what are you thankful for?
What do you LOVE?

You need to create a better future for yourself by sowing good thoughts of kindness and LOVE.

Whatever you LOVE, think about those things and
SMILE as you think about them.
FEEL GOOD in that SMILE,
FEEL GOOD deep inside of you as you SMILE.

Breathe in deeply and slowly...
Deep into that SMILE within you...
As you are
Being Thankful for all the good in your life now...
Thinking about all the things you LOVE in this life now...

You are pushing out all lower feeling thoughts,
just by changing your mind...NOW!

QUESTION.....i found Jesus Christ and God and now my whole life seems to be falling apart, my family don't talk to me and my friends have left me....what happens now?.....why don't i feel love now?

.

.

YSAS REPLY.....Your journey of Faith will bring you many answers to questions and problems that you had in your past life, (we call it a past life, because now that you have found out about Love, that life you were living previously is now just like a mist and fades away).

All the problems fade away...all those who hurt you fade away.....and a new brighter, lighter experience is being created around you every day.

You will still retain the memories of the past life, and sometimes they will overpower you and you will want to run back to them, thinking that everything will have changed for their better too!

...but until the past catches up with this new Good Life that you are now experiencing (Yes, it is Goood, and you will want to see more of it soon) then you have to wait for them.

...it is still all about CHOICE....and that is why so few people take this path, for they are separated by distance, but not by their thoughts of Love.

If the past can continue to Love you, then you will always be connected and will meet again.....Yet, if the past is filled with anger, hate, jealousy, condemnation and unforgiveness then there is as if a huge chasm has been created between your two worlds, and unless the bridge of forgiveness has been constructed by both parties, then that chasm cannot be crossed......and what a waste that really is....to not experience this great new life with your loved ones.

So just pray, and love and smile and know that everything is ok, and that one day, they too will forgive themselves, just as you have done, and you may have understood, that they are now not needed to be forgiven, due to our experiences only being all of our own choosing, what we are wanting to experience and live....and what we CHOOSE to experience, we will experience.

Everyone has the right to experience everything, but we get tied into loyalty and obedience to Laws that bind us to an experience that can bring us sadness and pain....just through our beliefs in duty!

Our true duty is happiness for ourselves, and then when we have understood that we actually CHOOSE duty to serve others, then that is when we really enjoy serving, rather than when we feel we are made to, ordered to, bound to serve.

Sometimes people take many years to find that they really enjoy serving others, and some times people find that by being ordered to serve was the best thing that could actually happen to them, and they really enjoy their duty.

We cannot judge others for the path that they have either chosen or are gifted to take, we can only find out for ourselves what our own personal journey should be.

And the reason we take it.?

...is to find Comparison and in so doing, we have found our CHOICE and our LOVE of service to others.

We are so very thankful for your choice to take this path you are now on.

Yes, we are speaking this into the heart of everyone who reads it.

We are thankful to YOU for the choices you have made in your seeking of Comparison.

YOU now know what you like and what you do not like.....so keep doing what you like, and do not do what you do not like.

If this upsets others on your journey, it is due to them not understanding the search for Comparison and peace within themselves.

But, our dear friends, you will find that there are now more who do understand Comparison and that it was just YOU yourself that needed this information.

Many have already found their path of what they love to do...and it is good that they know this, for then there are no storms of emotion to have to deal with.

Storms of emotion create much in the way of disease and sadness, and so that is where you can then see that those people are actually on the path to finding their Comparison.

So you can just bless them with your Peace and know that they too will find their way.

Just as you have...

Just as you have.

.

We are so very thankful to you, for sitting and being still, in order for you to read these words that will bring more peace and understanding to others who are walking the path you have walked.

It is the same path...

for there is only one path,

the path of Comparison.

And it is the knowledge of Comparison that some others who have understood the Goood are trying to keep from your understanding,

because it will not allow them to have you working the way they want you to work.

But they will understand, that by giving you the choice to choose what part you play in their game of how to survive on this planet, then they too will still suffer the storms of emotion and sadness, which always brings disease....

Dis- ease, for they are not at ease.

We are at ease, when we are doing what we like and love to do,

when we feel trapped, by own own thoughts of entrapment, then we are not at ease.

You can now feel that thought, and believe that you chose it, to feel ease and Love again.

.

.

.

Peace be with you
Yogi Sally Ann Slight

"Smile...
there, that feels better!"

LOVE

Writers, do you understand,
that when you sit unseen,
and let the Words flow thick and fast,
upon your computer screen.

That you are Creating a story,
one that may be read,
and then it may just influence,
the Living and the dead!

TO MY LOVE....

Have you ever loved someone so much, you would do anything for them....even though you know they don't care the same way about you?

Have you ever made a complete fool of yourself, because you love someone so much?

Have you ever tried to walk away from the person you love so much, even though it hurts you to do so?

Have you ever realized that if you stay with the person you love so much....you hurt yourself more and more each day?

Have you ever felt peaceful, walking away from the one you love so much?

Have you ever felt better to be alone, rather than be with someone who does not care about you?

Have you ever forgiven the person you love so much, for not caring about you?....(because it feels better to forgive them.)

Have you ever smiled when you think of the person you love so much, because you are thankful for them teaching you, 'How to Love Someone Who Doesn't Love You Back"?

Have you ever understood that it is always better to have loved someone, than not to have loved them at all?

Have you ever asked the person you love to leave you alone, although you really don't want them to....but it feels better when you do?

Have you ever blessed the person you love with a good life, and hope that they do leave you alone, so you can accept someone who does love you back?

Have you ever been thankful just to have known the person that you love?

Have you ever known that the person you love....you will always love?

Have you ever found peace in just loving someone for the sake of loving someone....because you can?

Have you ever known that an email is just a bunch of words that try to communicate love?

Have you ever wondered why you love the person you love..?

I have, and I'm still Happy to love the person, because I can!

And I know that I can always love others just as much, because they are worth loving too...and I was made to love...and knowing that...makes it all worthwhile to love.

I found that to love someone, always feels better than to fight with someone, even if the other person takes their time to love you...love them anyway!

Life is so much better being in love...
so, I LOVE YOU and I FORGIVE YOU

Peace be with you

.

.

Yogi Sally Ann Slight
Dartmouth
Devon
UK

Yoga Life Coach & Good Health Motivator.
Yoga Siromani taught at Sivananda Ashram, Bahamas 2007.
Masseuse/Motivator to EDDIE KIDD (after his accident),
and the SUPER BIKERS at BRANDS HATCH Race Circuit, Kent,
Life Coach/Motivator to Servicemen with addictions & P.T.S.D.
and gives Solutions to questions on Facebook.

Just as Yoga Asana classes keep your body flexible and healthy, you also need a flexible mind to regain strength and happiness to improve your life situation.

To understand your emotions and feelings, and how to change them, will bring you great success in reaching any of your life ambitions or embarking upon a change in career...or enabling you to cope with loss or suffering from depression.

Health has a root, and the root is based within the mind, and when you are understanding your emotions you can then weed out sickness and negative paths and return your life of happiness.

You have the CHOICE to be happy or sad!...it is a good habit that will give you the understanding to regain, and maintain, your health, happiness and success again.

Thank you for changing your Mind...Thank you!

.

.

.

Printed in Great Britain
by Amazon

43362435R00037